MONSTER POETRY

Fiendish Poems

Edited By Briony Kearney

First published in Great Britain in 2023 by:

YoungWriters® Est. 1991

Young Writers
Remus House
Coltsfoot Drive
Peterborough
PE2 9BF
Telephone: 01733 890066
Website: www.youngwriters.co.uk

All Rights Reserved
Book Design by Ashley Janson
© Copyright Contributors 2023
Softback ISBN 978-1-80459-993-8

Printed and bound in the UK by BookPrintingUK
Website: www.bookprintinguk.com
YB0560T

Foreword

Young Writers was created in 1991 with the express purpose of promoting and encouraging creative writing. Each competition we create is tailored to the relevant age group, giving each child the inspiration and incentive to create their own piece of writing, whether it's a poem or a short story. We truly believe that seeing it in print gives pupils a sense of achievement and pride in their work and themselves.

Our latest competition, Monster Poetry, focuses on uncovering the different techniques used in poetry and encouraging pupils to explore new ways to write a poem. Using a mix of imagination, expression and poetic styles, this anthology is an impressive snapshot of the inventive, original and skilful writing of young people today. These poems showcase the creativity and talent of these budding new writers as they learn the skills of writing, and we hope you are as entertained by them as we are.

Contents

Independent Entrants

Brooke Potter (10)	1
Jet-Leigh O'Riordan	2
Cali Mutter (8)	5
Serena Williams (11)	6
Marwah Qasir (10)	8
Belinda Kong (10)	10
Olutowo Omotoso (10)	12
Daniel Hamilton (10)	15
Clara Tempest (8)	16
Nieve Booty (11)	18
Simran Kaur (11)	20
Maya Pal (8)	22
Andikan Essien (11)	24
Ayeesha Imran (10)	26
Caterina Williams (12)	28
Sophie Hurst (12)	30
Shyla Miseer (12)	32
Cal MacPherson	34
Janna Oyedeji (10)	36
Xavia James-Musa	38
Adrian Obi	40
Sky Kwok (9)	42
Harine Wimalathasan (11)	44
Keshav Vasudevan (7)	46
Farah Karim (10)	48
Esther Akinwonmi-Pedro (9)	49
Andreea Maria Alexe (8)	50
Ayinoor Murray (10)	52
Zahra Ben-Saïd (8)	53
Muhammed Zeshan Aariz Wehvaria (7)	54
Tahir Aydin (10)	55
Amrutha Srikantham (10)	56
Thomas Durkin (8)	57
Cristina Alvanos (10)	58
Ditty Jones (8)	59
Brook Laycock (10)	60
Scarlett Impey (11)	61
Sanjena Rukshehan (8)	62
Siddhi Garg (11)	63
Dhara Wickramasekara (11)	64
Robyn Lindley (8)	65
Daniel Klu (11)	66
Ellie Kan (9)	67
Aina Dyandra (11)	68
Aycha Ben-Saïd (7)	69
Tanudi Vitharana (11)	70
Taslima Begum (12)	71
Maria Qasir (7)	72
Catherine Akinwonmi-Pedro (5)	73
Precious Adeyomoye (10)	74
Zuriel Oyedeji (8)	75
Ava Jay Swift (11)	76
Betty Rogers (9)	77
Sebbie Le Beron (8)	78
Luke Walters (8)	79
Amy Atkins (13)	80
Sophie Haslam (9)	81
Emily Hartness (10)	82
Henry Harris (8)	83

Ibstone CE Primary School, Ibstone

Iago Willcocks (9)	84
Jake Smith (8)	85
Julietta Anoszko (8)	86
Maisy Gomes (9)	87
Jacob Partridge (9)	88
Hawa Cotton (7)	89

Matilda Marshall (8)	90
Emmie Bishop (9)	91
Sonya Koptieva (10)	92
Mollie White (7)	93
Cihan Yilmaz (8)	94
Tom Shaw (8)	95
Surayyaa Zahid (8)	96
Sebastian Hawkins (8)	97
Ada Skene (9)	98
Jack Sullivan (9)	99

Lantern Academy, Ketley Bank

Eliza (9)	100
Elsa-Mai Darlington (7)	102
Emily (9)	103
Nadia Dziura (9)	104
Ella Smith (7)	105
Thales Palhano (9)	106
Sam Randall (7)	107
Logan H (9)	108
Theo A (9)	109
Mason Wright (8)	110
Tyler Hickman (8)	111
Jake Reynolds	112
Leo	113
Matei Cojocariu	114
Myla Nyantakyi	115
Theo Crawford (8)	116
Eliana Nyantakyi	117
Chester (7)	118
Kourtney (8)	119

Muirhouse Primary School, Motherwell

Mirrin Brownlie (9)	120
Taylor Clarke (9)	121
Olivia Speirs (9)	122
Ashton Warren (9)	123
Jenna Boyd (9)	124
Max Kerr (10)	125
James Smillie (9)	126
Caitlin Campbell (10)	127

Emily Lindsay (9)	128
Matilda Burnett (9)	129
Harry Brown (9)	130
James R (10)	131
Leland Dume (9)	132
Zak Gilfillan (10)	133
Lewis Boyle (9)	134

Selwyn Primary School, London

Maryam Bilal (9)	135
Amnah Hussain (9)	136
Kamran Fernandes (10)	137
Fatima Diop (9)	138
Keona-May Jones (9)	139
Nusaiba Miah (9)	140
Ammarah Iqbal (9)	141
Nijah Hossain (8)	142
Umar Chamdiya (10)	143
Ayaan Khan (8)	144

St Austin's Catholic (VA) Primary School, Stafford

Rosie Mellor (9)	145
Darcy Bickford-Kehoe (8)	146
Shreya Neelapala (9)	148
Niamh McNally (8)	149
Queenie Blewitt (9)	150
Talitha Chell (9)	151
Annabelle-Faye Watts (9)	152
Tobias Smalley (9)	153

The Poems

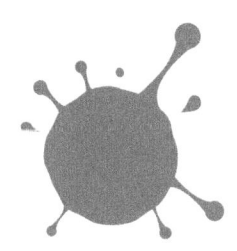

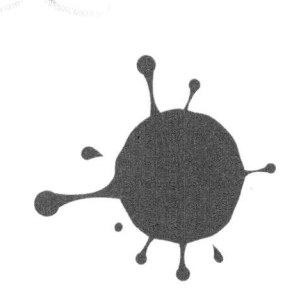

Strange New Pet

My mum finally said yes to a small, little pet,
I hadn't decided which one to get yet.
I could have got a bunny or a cute little cat,
But I wanted something more interesting than that.

A mysterious creature caught my attention,
He looked like he was from another dimension.
"Not that one!" Mum shouted from the next aisle,
But I had made my mind up, she could tell by my smile.

When I got home I noticed something weird,
My pet had grown a fluffy green beard.
His eyes were a shade of bright neon pink,
And after dinner, his breath started to stink.

As I fell asleep, I heard a strange noise,
And when I looked up, I saw lots of floating toys.
My pet was a monster, a magic one too!
I need some advice, what would you do?

Brooke Potter (10)

The Greedy Gid

The greedy Gid went out with friends
Invited for a meal
He scoffed an orange from the ground
And even ate the peel.

And once inside the restaurant
At home the Gid did feel
He ate chicken leg, with lots of veg
And pudding, what a deal.

The menu was a sight to see
And Gid was mesmerised
He licked the menu, front and back
And then apologised.

And then Gid ordered pizza
With ten ice creams, what a price!
Gid said, "I'll have the same again
Because it tasted nice."

And when Gid finished eating
It was not enough he ate

He looked around and took
A pork chop, from somebody's plate.

His friends sat in amazement
And the Gid, he was quite rude
He shouted to the waiters
"Hurry up! I want my food!"

"I've nearly finished eating
I will chomp this piece of beef
And when I've finished chomping
I would like to brush my teeth."

Now the food just kept on coming
And the table was a mess
So Gid turned around to talk
And spluttered food on someone's dress.

Now Gid was sitting happily
While eating egg-fried rice
He ate the food quite heartily
And then he ordered twice.

Gid sat among his friends
And piled the food upon his plate

And when the food was not on time
Gid shouted, "You are late!"
What a scene he did create!

The restaurant was busy
Waiters panicked in a state
And their mouths fell open when they saw
Gid licking around his plate
Throw him out! Don't hesitate
People thought, but did not state.

The greedy Gid said greedily
"I want! I want! I want!"
He was eating everything he saw
Inside the restaurant.

It was finally time to leave
The silent stares, if looks could kill
It wasn't very funny
When Gid's friends received the bill.

Jet-Leigh O'Riordan

Bad Luck Lumpy

This monster's hair is as long as a metre stick but at the same time it's surprisingly slick.
He eats minuscule mice as small as a marble - ugh, how disgusting!
He's old and grumpy, his name is Lumpy.
He has a three-legged cat, and its name is Stumpy.
He wears a pork pie hat perched on the top of his head.
But likes pink, fluffy pyjamas to wear to his bed.
He has a horrible, hairy honker, half a halo and horrendous horns.
He has beady little eyes, way too small for his size.
His den is dark, dank and quite dinky.
When he walks about, the floor goes boom and his bed is very bumpy...
He doesn't have much luck, poor old Lumpy.

Cali Mutter (8)

The Monster

Once you see it, you can't unsee it
Once it curses you, you can't be uncursed
Once it escapes your imagination, it can't be re-immersed
The monster, the fathoming, the heart-shatterer is real
And tonight it comes for his meal
Every night it returns
To feed off a fragment of fear
Every night I yearn
Not to hear the creaks as it's near
Not to see his ambery eyes burn
Not to think of him coming again
But he always comes, every night, every year
And then it only gets worse
I can feel his breath against my cheek
Bitter and solemn and cold
I can smell his presence, where he lurks away
In corners full of mould
And when he comes to suck my fear
I never feel so bold

One night I felt so terribly scared
And the monster came sneaking along
He sensed the fright inside my head
And started dangling his tongue
He stood next to my bed and lifted the covers
My eyes were closed, I couldn't look
I knew I was about to suffer
My teeth chattered, I trembled and shook
But even worse, he just picked me up
And didn't even touch me with his mouth
He just sucked at the air as if something was there
And then dropped me back in my house
After that the monster left, never to return
But I felt strangely empty, because he'd sucked my essence
Soon I realised I wasn't there anymore
I was just a ghostly presence that was easy to ignore
Now the monster goes and sucks elsewhere
But in my void of a heart, he is always there.

Serena Williams (11)

Sssh!

Beneath the bed where shadows creep,
A secret world where nightmares seep,
There dwell the monsters, dark and sly,
With glowing eyes and wicked sighs.

They wait in silence for the night,
To emerge from the darkness, filled with fright,
With gnarled claws and fangs so keen,
Their haunting presence, yet unseen.

When the moon is high and all is still,
They rise from depths with an eerie thrill,
Creaking floorboards, a warning sound,
As fear spreads through the room, so profound.

Under the bed, their kingdom lies,
A realm of darkness, where terror flies,
They slither and crawl, their forms grotesque,
Ready to torment and cause distress.

They whisper secrets in the ears,
Evoking nightmares, stoking fears,

Their chilling laughter fills the air,
As victims tremble, ensnared in their snare.

But do not let your spirit break,
For bravery is the shield you make,
Stand up tall, face the unknown,
And show those monsters they're overthrown.

With courage burning deep inside,
Banish the shadows where they hide,
Illuminate their fearsome might,
With a flick of the switch, bring forth the light.

For in the end, they're mere illusions,
Products of mind's wild confusions,
No monsters truly dwell beneath,
Just figments of imagination, beliefs.

So fear not those lurking beneath your bed,
Release the dread that's filled your head,
In the realm of dreams, monsters may abide,
But in the waking world, let love and courage preside.

Marwah Qasir (10)

There Once Was A Monster

There once was a monster,
With coal-black scales.
His blood-red eyes spoke of hunger,
Even heroes would tremble and pale.

Horns like a demon, tail like a dragon's,
A single breath could rattle a town.
And so, when the stars appear,
And the sun is down.

The people lock their doors,
Hoping that they won't be the monster's next meal.
He would then come, and roar as loud as he could,
But the people never thought of how the monster would feel.

How all he longed for was a family.
How all he wanted was a friend.
He had never thought of, ever dreamed of,
Making somebody's life end.

Then one day, a little girl,
Went outside at night.
She met the monster, talked to him,
And decided to make things right.

At first, no one believed her,
Then they came to trust her tale.
At last, they came up with a plan,
That they knew wouldn't fail.

So, that dusk, the monster came out,
From crying, red were his eyes.
But instead of a silent town,
He found a big surprise.

Everyone was out, laughing and saying, "Hi!"
Everyone smiled and shook his hand.
Everyone said sorry for casting him out,
Said that their land was now his land.

And so the monster lived there,
Until his last few days.
He had friends and family,
He was happy, in his own way.

Belinda Kong (10)

Ralph

Once I went out to the wood
But then all alone there I stood
So then I wondered if I should
Have even gone to that horrible wood.

Then I heard some growling
It sounded like something was strolling
Down this horrible wood
So then I went down falling.

I think it might have heard me
We'll just wait and see
Because I had just scraped my knee
Very, very badly.

So I started to bawl
A shadow came closer so I had to crawl
Away from the tall
Silhouette as fit as a wall.

But what I really saw looked like a dog
That had seven eyes and hopped like a frog

It came running and flying out of the fog
I thought, *I need to write this on my blog.*

I patted it on the head
"I'm going to take you home," I said
On the way home I read
The collar that said.

Ralph on it
And I will admit
I loved the dog
That was named Ralph.

So when I got home
I couldn't find Mum
So I just hid him in my room
But then I heard a scream.

Mum was in my room
She was pointing at Ralph
"What is that thing?" she asked
But before I could answer she said.

"Take it back from where it came from"
I replied, "No, I'm keeping it"

"Then you're taking care of it," Mum said
So I did.

But I tried really hard and it wasn't like a dog
It never listened to me
And sadly, very sadly
One day, Ralph just left me.

Olutowo Omotoso (10)

Monster Mayhem

M onsters watch you day and night
O vernight your dreams become reality
N eglected by the thoughts that surround you
S elected by the monsters and ghosts
T old different stories day by night
E erie sounds come from under your bed
R aced by your scary thoughts and dreams.

M eet them at the finish line at the back of your brain
A nchored by the support of your family
Y ou lie in bed with no one to help you
H elpless and foolish, your brain goes in spirals
E very single breath you take
M onsters wait for your screams to break.

Daniel Hamilton (10)

My Monster Friend

My monster friend,
All a gooey mess,
So gooey in fact,
He ruined my favourite dress,
I was running around,
Looking at my friend,
With his three eyes, three legs,
And arms sticking out his head,
"What can I do with you?
And how shall I clean up this mess?"
I looked at the broom then the goo and thought,
Well, Mum can fix my dress,
I picked up my broom,
And started to sweep,
The dirt swooshed around,
As I started to weep,
I looked at my friend and sobbed, "That's enough!
I don't know what's up with you,
But this is simply just too tough,"
I stared down at the goo,
And exclaimed sadly,

"You just do not feel my pain,"
I shouted loudly,
"A gooey mess,
A dirty shack,
And nearly,
Every shelf's been smacked,
With a gooey hand,
A sticky finger,
And the smell of stink always seems to linger,"
And my friend is not a friend anymore,
For I shoved him out and slammed the door,
But every day,
He seems to come back,
Skipping along,
To our gooey, dirty shack,
And those times I seem to let him in,
For he sweeps things up,
And stuffs rubbish in the bin,
You must think that these are chores,
But for us, it's a game,
And now those sweet sweet memories,
Seem to feel the same.

Clara Tempest (8)

Artina - The Monster On My Desk

Most kids hate these mythical creatures
Big sharp teeth, three eyes, uneven toes are just some of their nasty features
Yes, I am talking about monsters, big and small
Hiding in smelly bogs, creeping in between trees and under the beds, they crawl
But it was on a cool summer's night
I saw a very unusual sight
Because sitting on my desk was a sort of blob
Really no bigger than a doorknob
I tiptoed closer then I saw it was clutching a brush and a pot of paint
How strange, am I dreaming? I feel a bit faint
It had pencils for hair, scissors for wings and a tail made of glue
What is this creature, where did it come from and what shall I do?
It handed me a pen from its topknot of colour
It was so bright it made my neon pens look duller
We sat together for a while making doodles and random art

It was then I knew this little monster had a special place in my heart
But then I became tired and fell asleep in my chair
I woke up in shock to find she wasn't there
I cried and cried for hours upon end
Thinking that I'd lost my new friend
Then from my window a flash of light
It was extremely bright
Back from the Stationery Universe in space
With a huge smile on her face
Because she's here to stay
From then on we made art every day
Me and Artina best friends forever
We will never part I doubt ever!

Nieve Booty (11)

A Woven In Unexpected Monster

Undivided
Attention!
Focus!

It wants your whole attention.
It will *lure* you in
With eyes so *mesmerising*
It will envelop you with *worry, doubt*
And yet a certain *want*.

It will have you keep on coming back
With whispers of, "Everyone else is with me
You will be left out
You need me!"

It will fill your mind with a trance-like fog
It will make you oblivious to things that surround
It will make you forget
Time's blotting pen.

And yet it can be a thing of good
In a certain moderation
And it fills minds with information
A certain knowledge of the world.

It will fill your mind with doubt or with information
It will fill your mind with want or restraint
It will fill you with a false knowledge
Or it will fill you with a better understanding of the world.

Is this thing good or bad?
Well it is up to you to decide
For it is how you perceive it
And it depends on how you use it in your stride.

This thing is made of ones and zeros
Algorithms and more
And this thing can be beastly or good evermore
Social media.

Simran Kaur (11)

Blue

The sea is silent
It seems abandoned but restless
It has awoken from
Its bone-chilling sleep
But on May the fifth
It is free to creep
Skin as blue as Neptune
Eyes as red as a fresh river of blood
This beast fills man with dread
On the fifth of the fifth
As they go to bed
Deep under the sea where few venture
Leathery tentacles unfurl
Great big eyes blink open
Into the watery world
Eternal heartache burns inside him
Longing for love
To carry him away from revenge and despair
To soothe his sorrow and bathe him in peace
Many years ago, they were torn away
But what happened, I can not say

The horrendous moment still stings today
Torn away from heaven into war
Even though he's fierce
Hope is what he's looking for
Men don't believe, men don't care
They say long-lost love was never there
This happened once and it will happen again
This eternal torment must end
On the fifth of the fifth
The curse is shattered
For one night, he is able to roam on land
Sea and cliff
Bonded together
To make feeble sand
Terror reigns in the village
Until dawn breaks
Fateful fog descends
Making children quake
"Going up, up, up
Then the surface breaks
Staring at the town
Deciding mankind's fate."

Maya Pal (8)

The Monster In The Night

I had always dreamt of monsters
That would give me such a fright
But I'd never dreamt of a monster
That was such a funny sight!

With the lovely fur of a feline
And the thin, black wings of a bat
The little, fuzzy monster
Had the long, pink tail of a rat.

It came as I slept in my cosy bed
As I slowly drifted to sleep
But I wasn't expecting a small white thing
To gently begin to cheep.

This sound awakened me instantly
And I woke with a jolt of the head
Drowsily, I looked around my room
And once again sunk into my bed.

Although I didn't know it
The monster had crept toward me

And when, again, I awoke to its cheep
I spotted its tail but thought, it couldn't be!

And when I aroused the next morning
I felt something on my cheek
I turned to see the monster
Then I shook the house with a *shriek!*

"What is it?" said my mother,
Peeking around the door
But when I looked down again
The thing could be seen no more.

Andikan Essien (11)

A Troublemaker Monster

Help!
There's a monster in my kitchen,
I don't know what to do.
He's going through all my snacks and eating all my food!
Oh no!
The beady-eyed monster is climbing up my legs,
He drove me straight to the dining room and all the way upstairs.
Now look what he's doing!
He's lying on my bed and drawing on the walls,
I tried to say to him, "This bed is not yours!"
But all he did was gnarl and roar.
He takes my socks and hides my phone,
Into a secret place that only he knows.
This monster is cheeky and hard to control,
He even hides my toilet roll!
His fluffy body is as small as an ant,
He is mischievous, and his manners are scant.
He stole my wallet and spent my money,
On useless things like chocolate and honey!

This monster is chaotic,
And sometimes a little idiotic.
He chuckles and grins,
With food marks on his chin.
I know he's a troublemaker,
But he will always be my friend.
In the end, all that matters,
Is that we'll be together forever!

Ayeesha Imran (10)

A Monster

It's scary and it's frightening
Drains the colour from your face
Whitening.

Monsters will bite you, shred you to pieces
Just for something to chew.

They'll let your body go rotten
Waiting, drooling, to devour you
Now squishy and soft like cotton.

Monsters are unintelligent beasts
Cannot comprehend us
They growl and bark and do not speak.

According to the book, a monster is large and ugly
Frightening and imaginary
They are not people, they're creatures
A monster could even say that smugly.

But if a monster is imaginary
Ugly and large, says the dictionary

Who's this cute, small thing?
Furry, with two horns and one little wing.

So... maybe I am dreaming
But here's a monster, and I'm not screaming.

Perhaps some of those myths were wrong
And since these creatures are made up in your mind
They don't have to be scary, you might find.

Because here is a monster
And it's cute as heck!
I pick it up and cuddle it
Oh my gosh, it's so soft
Just beneath the neck.

Caterina Williams (12)

My Monster

This creature can be caring, kind and clever,
They're bananas but balanced, they're the best person ever.
They can be cuckoo, crackers and crazy,
But they are also lax, listless and lazy.
One day they could cry and keep to themselves,
And others, they shall shout and show their self.
They are angry and aggressive and all about attention,
But they are typically tender and love affection.
Haters will hate them and rip them in half,
Lovers will like them and make them laugh.
They turn green with envy or if they have the flu,
But when sorrowful and sad, they turn blue.
They turn red with anger if you don't share,
And pink if you give them a death stare.
If they chortle, the chuckle will often spread,
"Like an infection," people have said.
But this monster is mainly, mostly like you,
But they're different and delicate, distinctive from you.

This monster is mischievous, mad and messy,
This monster, in fact, is the marvellous me!

Sophie Hurst (12)

Am I Hallucinating?

My name
I can hear my name being whispered
But from who?
There is no one here or there or anywhere
There
A hand
A hand is perched on my shoulder
Though I cannot see it
I feel it as it rhythmically taps me
Pinky, ring, middle, index
Pinky, ring, middle, index
My name
There it is again
My name is whispered
Am I hallucinating?
Is this a dream?
A finger traces my spine and I see blood drip from behind me
Yet I am not wounded
Nor is it my blood
I ask myself again

Am I hallucinating?
I can hear it
This time it is not my name
The sound of a harp playing devilish tunes engulfs my room
And if I'm not hallucinating, then what could it be?
A monster?
Of course not, monsters aren't real
Are they?
Those two words were the last of that person
So I ask again
Am I hallucinating?

Shyla Miseer (12)

Bedtime

The monsters, they have one eye,
The monsters, they always lie,
The monsters, they stomp and shout,
Oh why, oh why, oh why.

The monsters, they have black teeth,
The monsters, they are very good thieves,
The monsters, they make you cry,
Oh why, oh why, oh why.

The monsters, they have long fingers,
The monsters, they aren't good thinkers,
The monsters, they steal your toys,
Oh why, oh why, oh why.

The monsters, they have green spots,
The monsters, they make bad plots,
The monsters, they have green fur,
Oh why, oh why, oh why.

The monsters, they scream and wail,
The monsters, they have short tails,
The monsters, they have sharp nails,
Oh why, oh why, oh why.

But...
When it is bedtime...

The monsters, they put on their PJs,
The monsters, they snuggle in their duvets,
The monsters, they cuddle their teddies,
Good night, good night, good night.

Cal MacPherson

Marvellous, Magical Monsters

In my world of marvellous monsters,
They come alive, one after another!
Not just one or two, oh my, no!
I have a whole collection that I show.
Each monster I create, you see,
Reflects a human like you and me.
One is kind and funny and sweet,
Just like my friend, an enjoyable treat.
Another has a two-sided face,
One side gracious, the other dark with no grace.
A mix of good and evil, a sophisticated blend,
Like the contradictions in some humans, my friends.
Don't limit yourself to just one monster, my friend!
In my mind, mysterious creatures are just around the bend.
They can be pretty, scary, naughty, or hairy,
Inspired by humans, so distinct and extraordinary.

So come and accompany me in this monster parade,
Where imagination and creativity never fade.
With every creation, an origin's uncovered,
In a world where magical monsters decipher.

Janna Oyedeji (10)

What Can It Be?

What can it be?
A fluffy, scruffy something hiding behind a tree.
Can you guess what it can be?
A lion, a frog, a stinky old hog?
What can it be?
Just what can it be?

It could be one million things, that I just can't see.
I can't forget that fluffy old thing.
Can it sing or does it have flying wings?

Blue and green should never be seen.
But what can I see?

The colour pink is very cool, what colour can it be?
What can it be?
Just what can I see?

Does it have twenty bendy arms with lots of charms?

Is it cute?
Is it cuddly?
Is it bubbly?

What can it be?

I have to see what's hiding behind that tree.
It's fluffy, scruffy and puffy with big googly eyes.
What can it be?
Just what can I see?

It's jumping out of the tree!

Xavia James-Musa

The Monster Under My Bed

In my bedroom,
There is a bed.
Not just any old bed,
It's a... monster bed.
And that's because,
There is a monster under my bed...
As I sleep, Melon the Monster,
The monster under my bed,
Is at work.
Whether he's jumping, running, hopping or skipping,
He never has breaks.
Today, he's in the kitchen.
Though he's not helping with the cooking,
Like a normal monster or person would do,
Because right now, Melon the Monster is...
Doing the dishes? Nope.
Fighting the Fridge Monster? Nope.
Stealing cookies from the cookie jar?
Nope, nope and nope.
So what is he doing you may ask?

Well, Melon is,
And this is a secret, promise not to tell anyone,
Feasting on all the food in the kitchen.
Yeah, that's pretty bad.
Oh well.
Guess they'll have to buy more food.
Right?

Adrian Obi

My Monster Pet

One day, I was making orange jelly
I put the jelly in the fridge carefully
And after some time
I heard some rumbling coming
From the fridge…

Guess what I found in the fridge?
A mouse? A skunk? A fox? A squirrel?
Oh no, no, no.
It was an orange, slimy, jelly-like monster
With eyes, a mouth, arms and legs!

It ran out of the fridge
Jumped onto the table
And stuck itself to the ceiling
I had to bring it down from the table
It was very slippery and squishy

It jumped out of the window into the garden
And suddenly curled into a ball
It rolled around and all
Got covered in grass quickly

It looked like a tennis ball!

I washed the grass off it gently
It said, "Thanks!" politely
Surely, it made my day
I looked after this monster like a pet
And decided to call it Jelly-Pete!

Sky Kwok (9)

Agramon

A monster, a monster
Dark and terrible to see
It attacks you when you have no armour
It makes you a suicidee
It turns into what you fear the most
Maybe even a ghost.

But what is it? What is it, you ask?
It is fear, fear so great - *Agramon*
He wears a deceiving mask
Your mind spiralling with fear will get a concussion
Agramon is fear
Fear is Agramon.

When faced, only pain will be brought
Death upon the one who tries to confront it
Everything will have been for naught
If only you had struck the first hit...
You would not have gone to the pits of hell
You never had time to say farewell.

He is unbeatable
Many have succumbed to Agramon
Millions have died trying to defeat him
Even when an angel is summoned
Fear always wins
With all his sins.

Harine Wimalathasan (11)

Monster Mystery

I was drifting off to bed
I heard the floorboard creak
I saw something red
It had a giant curvy beak

My mother said,
"It's clothes hanging from a cupboard
Don't be a coward"

I entered the hall
I saw the wall frames shake
It was something giant and tall
Oh, for goodness' sake!

My father said,
"It's the wind wobbling the wall frame
A monster is not the one to blame"

I went to the kitchen for a drink
I heard the vessels rattle and cling
There was something creeping out of the sink
It looked bright and bling

My brother said, "It's just the chopstick
Don't be dramatic"

Do you think there is a monster in my house?
Or was it just a mouse?

Keshav Vasudevan (7)

Did I See A Friendly Monster?

I am a princess with my gem-made crown
Today I saw a monster hanging in town
With blue-striped arms and a fluffy coat
That fur won't stand the breeze on a boat

His tail waggled just like a cute spaniel puppy
Its eyes were big enough to fit a single guppy
I peer over, did I just hear the sound of cries?
Then it sat down, and a frown started to rise

I scurry over and start to ask what's the matter?
It did tell me what was wrong and we had a chatter
Apparently, the lonely monster has no friends,
Should we help, since we can do some amends?

Let's be this friendly monster's forever friend
I hope all happy emotions are what we'll send.

Farah Karim (10)

Winky And I

My monster likes the sun,
And is loved by everyone
He sits by the window side,
And when it's bathtime he likes to hide.
At lunch he doesn't eat much,
He doesn't make such a fuss.
He doesn't have manners, but that is okay,
At least afterwards, we can play.
At playtime we have lots of fun,
Toys and playsets for everyone.
Sometimes we make such a mess,
But really, I think that's the best.
Finally, it's bedtime now,
Grab your teddies, or your plush cow.
Rest, rest, that is all we need,
Now close your eyes and go to sleep...

Esther Akinwonmi-Pedro (9)

Fair Of The Wolf

When they built my house
The builders forgot
Or they left it on purpose
A wolf in the attic of the house

When we moved in
I had no idea
About the wolf in the attic
Which grew
And grew
Feeding on spiders

I think so though
He went out in the evening
I happened to hear
A strange and scary noise
From the attic of the house

One day
When I took my toys to the attic
I saw him
And scared to death

I read quickly on Google
How to kill a monster

I read like a beast
It must be lured out
In the sun
Under the heat of summer
On a scorching day

That's how I proceeded
And the fierce wolf
It simply exploded
In thousands and thousands of toys!

Andreea Maria Alexe (8)

Sockie - The Sock Monster

Hello! I'm Sockie.
I look pretty normal, right?
Except that in my case,
Appearances are deceiving.
I'm a monster!

My socks look vibrant and long
But beware of the pong!
Don't get too close, your nose will thank you.
You saved their life
And perhaps yours too.

They never get a wash,
As I hate the sound of the swish and swosh.
Save your socks, before the clock tocks.
Trust me!
Smelly is something you will not be.
Just me, because I'm a monster,
I'm Sockie, the sock monster!

Ayinoor Murray (10)

My Monster

My monster is scary, big and hairy.
But to me, he is kind and generous.
As he causes mischief to make me smile.
Sneaking in houses and making people scream.
Like monsters on TV, he feeds on their fear.
But he only needs to do it once a year.
The rest is for fun,
As we watch people run.
He can't stand in the sun,
So night-time is when we make a scream.
Halloween Night is our favourite night of the year because we like to cause mischief together.
My scary monster friend will be with me to the very end!

Zahra Ben-Saïd (8)

I Am A Monster, Found In...

I don't drive a monster truck
I am not yuck
When I chew food it sounds like a cluck
My idea is taken as a shuck.

You won't see me in the dark
You won't see me in the park
When the dog sees me, it barks
My name is Shark
But I don't shine like a spark.

I don't know if I am scary
But everyone calls me hairy
I behave warily
I eat cherries.

You can find me in a school
I teach children to make them fools
I am a monster
Because I am a teacher.

Muhammed Zeshan Aariz Wehvaria (7)

The One And Only Jigglywoo

Your great jelly pies I loved so much.
Oh, why do you have to go now, Jigglywoo?
Your soft fuzzy hair filled me with great delight.
I might say goodnight.
Those bittersweet memories of those figs and cranberries,
I always picked them off, anyways.
You better come back right this instance,
Or else I'll be joining you in Valhalla tonight.
Just one more day, shall I say Jigglywoo.
For sure, it would make the day.
I must admit you were quite the package, hey.
But it was good while it lasted.
You could say so...

Tahir Aydin (10)

My Emotional Monster

My emotional monster is called Sally,
Sometimes she acts really silly,
Once my mum woke to find,
A Halloween toy of a horse's hind,
The next thing my naughty monster did,
Was pretend to fly on a saucepan lid,
Once everyone was sad,
She cheered us up and we played in the sand,
But now I'm old but will never forget,
The great times we had,
Growing up,
She started to stop,
Till the chart line dropped,
And now has a house where she now lives,
She has a life but,
Still wonders whether she would ever fly on a saucepan lid.

Amrutha Srikantham (10)

The Diary Of A Monster

My name is Zog
And I am writing on a log
A story about our strange days
And the games that we play

Here in our home we monster's play dog oo do
Where your dog, Lou or Stu, chases us to the loo

Up on the roof
We monsters eat ice cream
With dots that are all colours; red, purple
and green

We like to cook in the kitchen and tasty things
to eat
Like mud pies with our secret ingredient...
stinky feet

Thank you for listening to what we monsters do
Which was written by Zog Coocoo.

Thomas Durkin (8)

Unicorns

Fearless creatures sprinting through the earth
Every second, one is giving birth
Riding, sliding, gliding through the skies
Even though they are brave, hiding is advised
Many are shy, many are brave
Some of them are cheeky, and some do behave
Unicorns are never considered slaves
Even if they are sad, their smile will be glad
Even if they are mad, they will never act bad
There's a lot to say, as unicorns brighten up my day.

Cristina Alvanos (10)

Cake

Monsters are creatures under the bed.
Monsters are creatures, not a nightmare in your head.
Monsters wait till you're fast asleep.
Monsters then run down the stairs, or should I say creep?
Monsters look at what you bake.
Monsters hope its chocolate cake.
Monsters love your cake.
So that's why you need to stay awake.
You're probably wondering how I know this stuff.
And that's because I'm a monster and you're next on my list.

Ditty Jones (8)

My Strange Pet

Today I'm getting a new pet
Hip hip hooray
I chose one that's fluffy and grey
I think it's cute, okay?
But one night I heard a howl
So I got up and my pet was gone

The next morning
I went through the woods to look
All I found were dead deer
And some chickens near
I then felt scared
Because I had brought a beast to the east
So I started to run for my life
But suddenly everything went black
And the last thing I heard was a howl.

Brook Laycock (10)

The Wonder Of The Magic Of Chomp Chomp

There's a dragon that loves to eat and that's where it gets its name from, Chomp Chomp.
For years people cheered when Chomp Chomp came out of its wonderful, colourful and powerful cave that *no one* dared to go near.
Besides that, Chomp Chomp has a lovely life.
It has light hair (really bright pink) that might have magic when you touch it.
It's got yellow skin and got loads of limbs and that's what Chomp Chomp looks like.

Scarlett Impey (11)

Jewl The Monster

Jewl, Jewl
You are never cruel
And you are as soft as wool
You are my friend
To the very end
And you and I like to bend
You are pink
And like to get feathers and ink
And see if people say congratulations
For our new creations
For generations
You have a friend called Blue
And he likes to make animal noises like moo
Jewl says, "And we like to be with all of you
You just wait and see."

Sanjena Rukshehan (8)

My Bestie Tings!

My scientific friends,
I hope you could spend
A little time reading this,
It certainly isn't something you wanna miss!
It's about a mermaid with wings
Called Tings.
She has wild hair,
But oh, she doesn't care!
She has red eyes and light green skin
And also a very wide grin!
She eats only figs
And also big, fat pigs.
She loves me
And I love her too, you see.
We're besties forever
And ever and ever.

Siddhi Garg (11)

Beast Of Flames

Scavenging the sky,
Looking for a meal,
Oh, mighty beast,
We beg you mercy.

Rampaging the ground,
Burning everything in its path,
Oh, vicious beast,
We beg you mercy.

Shaking the planet,
As hot as the sun,
Oh, king of all the universe,
We beg you mercy.

Wrecking my planet,
Gulping down all living beings,
Oh, nightmare,
Become a dream!

Dhara Wickramasekara (11)

My Monster Joe

My monster's name is Joe
He loves to wear bows
He has spots on his feet
He is a delight to meet
He has stripes on his back
And eats cherries for a healthy snack
His favourite bird is a dove because it rhymes with glove
He has wings but cannot sing
He doesn't live in my house, he lives with a mouse
He is quite small but I am tall
That's goodbye, so he must fly.

Robyn Lindley (8)

A Friend Or A Foe

I sense something in the air,
A terrifying creature that fills my heart with fear.
I run for my life
As I sense a beast with strife,
I run and run, for we are not done.
But there is my fate,
A creature that gives me no escape,
Then I will be known as late.
However, I am confused
For the monster is amused.
The shiny teeth of thee,
The face the shape of a tree.
I glare not in fear,
For that one is not troublesome.

Daniel Klu (11)

The Dangerous Dragon

I once saw a dragon with gleaming white fangs
What a fierce beast!
It easily killed with a twitch of its claw
And food went quickly down its humongous maw
But super strong scales protected it from harm
When soldiers realised they couldn't fight it they shrieked in alarm!
So you better be warned of that hungry dragon with merciless eyes
Or it will gulp you up or put you in a pie.

Ellie Kan (9)

Monstrous Mist

M ists of mighty dream
O f a beastly monster scream
N ot this time, I shall not hide
S oft chimes of misery have opened my eyes wide
T remendous shadows darken the room
R evolting stench as a dead sparrow pierces into the gloom
O h, leave me alone!
U nafraid of the beasts unknown
S lightly scary, but not as daring as me.

Aina Dyandra (11)

My Monster

My mysterious monster has massive round eyes
He has enormous razor-sharp teeth
And he has a huge black mouth
He has light blue fur.

My monster has a dark blue button nose
His arms are long like noodles
His legs are fat like tree trunks
His body is gigantic.

My monster lives underneath my stairs
Don't worry though, he has a pillow and blanket too.

Aycha Ben-Saïd (7)

The Monster Under My Bed

A pair of eyes,
Glaring right at me,
Under my bed,
Grabbing on to me.
Will it kidnap me and take me to its lair?
Will it eat me up and store my corpse?
Will it grab my toes and rip them off my feet?
I hide under the blankets,
Closing my eyes.
What if the monster freezes me,
Just like Medusa did?
I wake up at dawn,
To my mother's voice.
Oh, thank you, Lord,
It's just a dream.

Tanudi Vitharana (11)

The Monster Under My Bed

There's a monster under my bed
Always poking at my head
Making a groggy type of noise
The sound of my fear is what it enjoys
Its giggles are devious
I wish it was how it was in the previous
Its identity is mysterious
And it makes me feel delirious
I want her to leave, I know I'll never miss her
But my parents keep calling it my little sister.

Taslima Begum (12)

Skumpy The Monster

My friend Skumpy lives in my room with me.
He watches me with his big eyes all the time.
When he smiles at me I can see his big yellow teeth.
He has big, hairy, green hands and hairy, long fingers that always wave at me.
He eats paper and books all day, his tummy is so big.
He eats all my homework and reading books, I don't know what to do.
I think he doesn't like school.

Maria Qasir (7)

Baddy Alien

Baddy alien is a scary, silly and fun alien.
In the mornings, he had his breakfast
But after he finished it he felt sick.
He turned green like he always did.
When we were about to go to the party,
He got really sick
And we had to not go to the party.
I had to give him medicine
And then tucked him into bed!

Catherine Akinwonmi-Pedro (5)

Riddle Riddle

I have four legs
I am light brown
I live in the jungle
I can roar
I hunt during a storm
My group is called a pride
I sleep twenty-four hours a day
I can leap thirty-six feet
I weigh thirty stone
I am between 3.5 and 4 feet tall
I like running for fun
I can camouflage
I am fearless
What am I?

Answer: A lion.

Precious Adeyomoye (10)

The Gemi Monster

I love my monster
He is fast, strong, noble and bold
I also love him because he is always protecting me
And every time things get wrong
All I see is the monster helping me
I dearly love my monster
And he loves me too
I wish everyone had this kind monster
Because he would also like you!

Zuriel Oyedeji (8)

The Monsters In My Room

I heard them creep into my room,
Each step they took made a boom!
They looked scary,
I wanted to fight, but I was weary.
They seemed loud,
They seemed proud.
But under all that fur,
They were afraid of a simple purr
That came from my cat,
Hiding below my hats.

Ava Jay Swift (11)

Monstertastic

My monster has green skin
My monster has one eye
My monster has one arm
My monster has one leg
My monster has one eyelash
My monster has one ear
My monster has one eyebrow
My monster has lots of hair
I love my monster.

Betty Rogers (9)

Cheetah

A kennings poem

Meat muncher
Day hunter
Speed runner
Lonely liver
Black dotter
Eagle-eyed spotter
Fierce prowler
Graceful growler
Magnificent mammal
Clever camouflager
Decade survivor
Dangerously endangered.

Sebbie Le Beron (8)

Son Of The Boiling Isles

I come from the boiling isles
I was adopted by Eda, the owl lady
I am diminutive in size and very cute
But beware of my shadows
For they are fearsome
I will terrify you
But it is just a joke
I am King!

Luke Walters (8)

My Monster

A furry monster, one eye
That sounds like a lie
There is a monster under there
Go away from where
I am not lying, I am honest, Pete
It has big feet
So huge and furry with green claws
The biggest claws I have ever seen.

Amy Atkins (13)

Monsters Can Be Different

A diamanté poem

Monster
Cuddly, cute
Beaming, creating, helping
Imagination, positivity, devil, horns
Creeping, sneaking, lurking
Troublesome, nightmare
Monster.

Sophie Haslam (9)

The Clab

C ontinuously going crazy
L onely without me
A ncient creatures no one knows
B rilliantly orange Clabs.

Emily Hartness (10)

The Monster

Satanic messiah
The smell of missiles on fire
Rising higher and higher
A beat of wings...
Silence.

Henry Harris (8)

Monsters Are Scary

M arvellous with his shiny hair,
O ptimistic when making friends,
N aughty when making jokes,
S orry because of his eyes,
T remendous spelling,
E xcited when playing games,
R esurrected from the dead,
S uspicious in crimes,

A nxious when talking to people,
R idiculous when he jokes,
E legant legs,

S uper good at writing,
C ool when he drives his motorbike,
A mazing at school,
R eading books,
Y elling at bullies.

Iago Willcocks (9)
Ibstone CE Primary School, Ibstone

Pabba And Spike

2000 years ago, the man hit the Earth,
And loads of monsters came,
Some of the monsters were friendly,
And some of them were bad,
In the future, one monster was still alive,
His name was Pabba,
Pabba was nice,
He didn't harm people,
But some people think he's terrifying and mean,
Because he's got scary spikes on his body,
And four eyes and sharp teeth,
He likes to play hide-and-seek with his friend Spike,
His friend Spike is invisible,
So Pabba can never find him.

Jake Smith (8)
Ibstone CE Primary School, Ibstone

The Mischievous Squiggle

One day, at school,
I was doing art
I saw a monster out of the window.
I thought that it would come in
And what's what happened.
He was *sooo* cross
He smacked his feet on the paint.
The paint was all over the classroom
I chased him out of the window
Through the bushes
He led me to my home.
"How did you bring me here?" I said
All he did was ignore me...

Julietta Anoszko (8)
Ibstone CE Primary School, Ibstone

My Monster Is Friendly

When my monster pops up to play,
It's usually evening, not the day.
Whenever I am scared, he comes to town
And sees my smile is upside down,
When I am upset, it affects his day,
But when I am happy, he goes away,
I feel calm when he is here,
He takes away all my fear,
His name is Stitch the friendly monster,
When he visits I am sad no longer.

Maisy Gomes (9)
Ibstone CE Primary School, Ibstone

Monster Jump

I was walking along, one fine afternoon,
When a human-sized monster jumped out of the blue,
It had five pretty eyes and a couple of antennae,
It had five foul teeth and a pair of wings,
And so I decided to name him Bing,
I put him in my bag the very next day,
And then he saw his prey,
So he jumped into a pile of hay,
So I left Bing that very same day.

Jacob Partridge (9)
Ibstone CE Primary School, Ibstone

Monster

M ucky,
O nly one left,
N ice,
S illy,
T ragic,
E xciting,
R eally fun.

My monster is called Fuzzy,
He's really fun, no way he'll be sad,
He's always there,
And makes up games when I'm bored,
My monster lives in the garden.

Hawa Cotton (7)
Ibstone CE Primary School, Ibstone

Merscail And Me

Me and Merscail are the best of friends,
We play forever, our fun is never done,
We never fight, we could play all day,
And we could play all night,
She eats the bad, so we are mostly good,
But she can be mischievous like Robin Hood,
We are different but we are friends,
And that will never end.

Matilda Marshall (8)
Ibstone CE Primary School, Ibstone

Tickle Monster

M agnificent monster, you will always be my
O verall friend, you bump your head,
N ever, never break your head,
S top, stop when I tell you to stop,
T ickle and tickle, please don't stop,
E ver and evermore,
R emember me, remember you.

Emmie Bishop (9)
Ibstone CE Primary School, Ibstone

Penny

M y monster is called Penny,
O r sometimes smelly Bob,
N o one likes to sit with him,
S o he lives inside a log,
T he children like to tease him and see him alone,
E very day he cries, it must be sad to be,
R eal like Penny.

Sonya Koptieva (10)
Ibstone CE Primary School, Ibstone

Sky Monster

Sonya and I, climbing high,
To get to fly in the sky,
But oh! We have got stuck in the tree,
Climbing down, but fell down,
I got down and helped her up,
Off we go, into the park
To feed the ducks,
And give them bread,
Sonya the monster has a sore head.

Mollie White (7)
Ibstone CE Primary School, Ibstone

Doomfoot

M y monster is called Doomfoot
O nion-smelling monster
N obody goes near him because he smells
S cary like thunder
T alons as sharp as razors
E veryone is scared of him
R acing through the town.

Cihan Yilmaz (8)
Ibstone CE Primary School, Ibstone

Tim The Nice Monster

Tim is strong
Tim is gigantic
Tim is colourful
His favourite colour is red
Tim is nice
He likes mice
Tim has lice
Tim loves giraffes
Big and small
He loves them all
This is Tim the monster.

Tom Shaw (8)
Ibstone CE Primary School, Ibstone

Monster

M y monster is called Stitch,
O nly cuddles his favourite teddy,
N o one likes his teddy,
S titch feels sad,
T eddy feels sad,
E verybody says sorry,
R emember this.

Surayyaa Zahid (8)
Ibstone CE Primary School, Ibstone

The Ooger Booger

Blobey eats the most scared kids.
If you see him, don't be scared or he'll
Eat you for a meal
Slime and snot he leaves behind.
Don't you dare step on it
Or he will do this!

Sebastian Hawkins (8)
Ibstone CE Primary School, Ibstone

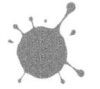

A Monster's Day

The monster walked to school,
The monster went to the loo,
The monster worked and worked,
The monster ate a child for lunch,
And then the monster went home.

Ada Skene (9)
Ibstone CE Primary School, Ibstone

My Monster

There was a monster called Joe Biden
Who was in the bin,
Jumped out at people,
And said goodbye to the people!

Jack Sullivan (9)
Ibstone CE Primary School, Ibstone

Hostile Crooked Man

The deformed, murderous killer appears rapidly from his dishevelled dwelling,
He sneakily crawls through the colossal, eerie forest,
Like a shadow, he shifted across the damp ground,
He is Hades from the underworld,

The deformed, murderous killer sneaks effortlessly into a secluded basement,
He secretly hides in the storage boxes,
He's as sneaky as a cat trying to catch its prey,
He is a TNT box waiting to erupt,
Quick as a flash, he strikes his target!

The deformed, murderous killer snatches the helpless prey,
He ravenously devours their slimy gooey brains,
As mercilessly as a ferocious lion,
He is a cannonball launching in the air,

The deformed, murderous killer teleports with his brim-full, crooked tummy,
He returned to his dishevelled dwelling,

He is as fat as a hippopotamus,
He is an ultimate machine that never needs a rest,
Will you be his next victim?

Eliza (9)
Lantern Academy, Ketley Bank

The Terryfing Monster

My silly, naughty little monster is hiding behind the huge bed,
He has disgusting, dirty teeth that need to be cleaned,
He is as red as the hot sun.

My silly, naughty little monster is under the chair,
He has ugly, scary skin,
He has bloody, scary legs,
He is as silly as a monkey.

My silly, naughty little monster is creeping on top of the staircase,
He has a huge, gigantic mouth with six pointy teeth,
He has an evil, creepy, strong laugh that will scare any children,
He is as loud as a bird.

My silly, naughty little monster is happy and he is jumping around the bedroom,
He has a pointy nose with a pink spot,
He is as silly as a clown.

Elsa-Mai Darlington (7)
Lantern Academy, Ketley Bank

The Bloody Devil

The annoyed, bloody devil furiously punched at the door,
He silently dashed through the malicious, gigantic school,
He has sharp, dreadful claws just like a slashing chamber machine,
He is a difficult creature sent from the underworld.

The annoyed, bloody devil travels to the dripping, bloody school,
He sneakily creeps out of the cupboard, ready to attack,
He is as sneaky as a ninja,
He is an evil creature.

The annoyed, bloody devil creature attacks an innocent child,
He tears up its skin whilst eating its disgusting, horrible brains,
He is as disgusting as a demon,
He is as feisty as a living creature.

Emily (9)
Lantern Academy, Ketley Bank

The Outraged Lightning Monster

The intimidating, outraged killer disappeared to his apartment and opened his eyes,
He quickly dashed through the foggy, dark graveyard,
Like a dragon from Hell, he prowled in the dark,
He is as quiet as a teddy bear.

The intimidating, outraged killer disappeared to his apartment and opened his eyes,
He secretly hides in the trees like a dragon in the basement,
He is your worst nightmare every time you are alone.

The intimidating, outraged killer disappeared into his gloomy apartment,
He quickly dashed towards a terrifying doll,
He stared at it like a jaguar watches his prey,
He is a doll-killing machine.

Nadia Dziura (9)
Lantern Academy, Ketley Bank

Killran The Malicious, Hostile Killer

The malicious, hostile killer growled through his sharp teeth,
He teleported to a mysterious, foggy dimension,
He is like a bull raging at someone,
He is mad as a demon,

The malicious, hostile killer was rolling like he had rollerskates on,
He quietly rolled through the sewers,
He was like the devil getting ready to kill someone,
It was like he was possessed,

The malicious, hostile killer climbed out of the sewer and crawled into the town,
He went into a girl's bedroom,
Then he burned her,
He was like the fire king,
He is a killing machine,

Watch out!

Ella Smith (7)
Lantern Academy, Ketley Bank

The Malevolent Triple Eye

The malevolent, alarming murderer furiously slashed a mysterious dwelling,
He quickly hissed through a deadly, noisy temple,
He is as gloomy as the dingy midnight,
He is a killing machine.

The malevolent, alarming murderer secretly flew to the most popular city in England, London,
He is as silent as a cat trying to catch his prey,
He is the sun waiting to see the people burn.

The malevolent, alarming murderer secretly eats a cheerful, innocent little girl,
He is as malicious as a movie villain,
He is a demon from the underworld.

Thales Palhano (9)
Lantern Academy, Ketley Bank

The Exterminating Malicious Machine

The hostile, murderous, malicious killer was scanning the land for his breakfast,
The monster is like a spooky, gigantic dragon,
The monster is a fire-breathing dragon!

The hostile, murderous, malicious killer teleported into the child's bedroom,
Its breath smelt like rotting meat left in the sun for days,
He is the ultimate machine that never needs to sleep.

The hostile, murderous, malicious killer violently attacks a tiny child,
He is as deadly as a poisonous spider,
He is the Hulk,
Did the child make it out?

Sam Randall (7)
Lantern Academy, Ketley Bank

Hydra Laser Dragon

The hostile, intimidating hydra dashed through gloomy caves,
He violently slashed through tall, stable buildings,
He is as angry as a raging man,
He is a demon.

The hostile, intimidating hydra flew over an innocent, sleeping village,
He quickly flew into tall, wide skyscrapers,
He is as silent as a mouse,
He is a soldier.

The hostile, intimidating hydra violently attacks its prey,
He chomps a velociraptor,
He is as loud as a compactor,
He is the evil devil,
Will you be its next victim?

Logan H (9)
Lantern Academy, Ketley Bank

The Pitch-Black Killing Machine

The hostile, murderous killer scanned for his cave,
He sneakily dashed to a pitch-black, quiet child's bedroom,
He was as quick as a cheetah,
He is the devil.

The hostile, murderous killer flew over a sleeping village,
He silently crept into a bedroom,
He is as terrifying as a demon,
He is an evil monster.

The hostile, murderous killer sneakily creeps around the house,
He viciously attacks the terrified victim,
He is as terrifying as a vampire,
He is your worst nightmare.

Theo A (9)
Lantern Academy, Ketley Bank

The Malevolent, Malicious Dragon

The alarming, hostile killer slashed powerfully through the door,
He sneakily sprinted through the spine-chilling, eerie graveyard like a scary demon sent from Hell,
He is a mythical creature sent from the underworld.

The alarming, hostile killer slashed powerfully,
He patiently waits in the ghostly graveyard,
He is as sneaky as a mouse,
He is an ultimate machine that never needs to rest.

The alarming, hostile killer teleported to the school,
He violently slashed a teacher's throat.
Is he your worst nightmare?

Mason Wright (8)
Lantern Academy, Ketley Bank

The Hostile Killing Machine

The malevolent, malicious monster is a murderous monster,
He transformed miserably inside the cold, white hallway,
He was hungry, so was as furious as King Henry VII,
He is a mythical creature.
The malevolent, malicious monster appears in the classroom,
He swooped effortlessly through the room,
He was as high as a bird,
He is a ninja.
The malevolent, malicious monster is now hiding in the staff room,
He is secretly inside the cupboard,
He is as still as a statue,
He is a statue.

Tyler Hickman (8)
Lantern Academy, Ketley Bank

The Emergent, Malicious, Malevolent Hydraulic Killing Machine

The withering, crimson monstrosity slashed hastily at the wall,
He quickly swooped through the spine-chilling, eerie graveyard,
Digging up the bones rapidly and eating them like a dog,
He is a demonic spirit travelling through dimensions, destroying worlds.

The withering, crimson monstrosity transformed rapidly,
Motionlessly standing in the dim, looming shadows,
He is as sneaky as a mouse,
He is a statue waiting for people to innocently walk by.

Jake Reynolds
Lantern Academy, Ketley Bank

Death Sea Monster

The murderous, malicious sea monster scanned the ocean,
He sneakily swam over to the old, giant bridge,
He is as scary as the devil,
He is the ocean king.

The murderous, malicious sea monster appears under the bridge,
He is as tall as a tree,
He is a shark.

Someone walked over the bridge,
He snatched them,
He ate them,
Rushed to the sewer to escape.

Leo
Lantern Academy, Ketley Bank

The Deadly Killer Machine

The deadly, murderous killer slashes furiously at buildings,
He sneakily dashed through the midnight, foggy graveyard,
He sprinted as fast as a cheetah,
He is your worst nightmare, appearing every time you are alone.

The deadly, murderous killer teleports to the city,
He violently glitches because he needs to kill,
He is as furious as a bull,
He is a deadly machine.

Matei Cojocariu
Lantern Academy, Ketley Bank

The Exterminating Man

The malicious, murderous killer slashed hastily at the wall,
He quickly dashed through the gigantic, enormous wardrobe,
He is as green as the Hulk,
He is an ultimate machine that never needs to rest.

The malicious, murderous killer teleported to the school,
He slowly hides in the staffroom,
He is as sneaky as a fox,
He is your worst nightmare.

Myla Nyantakyi
Lantern Academy, Ketley Bank

The Frightening Hostile Dragon

The frightening, hostile dragon slashed furiously with his sharp claws,
He silently crept through an enormous, aged house,
He dashed as fast as the Flash,
He is a killing machine,

The frightening, hostile dragon saw a kid in the large bedroom,
He quietly strolled up the crooked, old staircase,
He went as fast as a person drinking coffee,
He is never going to stop.

Theo Crawford (8)
Lantern Academy, Ketley Bank

The Malicious Shadow Monster

The monstrous, malicious monster flashed powerfully,
He quietly dashed through the eerie, spooky graveyard,
He is as furious as Henry VIII,
He is a demon monster from the underworld.

The monstrous, malicious monster glided effortlessly,
He carefully sneaked through the graveyard,
He is as quiet as a ninja,
He is a sneaky hunter.

Eliana Nyantakyi
Lantern Academy, Ketley Bank

My Monster

My silly little monster is jumping on the bed,
He has yellow, little, sharp teeth,
He has filthy, stained skin,
He is as orange as the sun.

My silly little monster is hiding under the stairs,
He has dirty, slimy toenails,
He has a silly, clown laugh,
He has strong, big arms.

Chester (7)
Lantern Academy, Ketley Bank

The Malicious Monster

The hostile, murderous monster hissed at the malicious, dark demons,
He sneakily dashed through the midnight air,
He is as sneaky as a hissing cat,
He is a killing machine.

Kourtney (8)
Lantern Academy, Ketley Bank

Fluffy's Poem

My monster went on a walk through the beach,
He enjoyed it,
He met his friend, Cookie,
They walked together,
They had so much fun,
While they were walking, they heard the waves splashing really fast,
They jumped in the ocean and swam like fish,
They had the best time ever,
After a while, they got tired and got out and dried off,
When they were dry, they had a sleepover,
And they had the best time ever.

Mirrin Brownlie (9)
Muirhouse Primary School, Motherwell

Cookie's Poem

It was my birthday,
I went for a walk on the beach,
I met my friend Fluffy,
We walked together,
Me and Fluffy got tired,
So we jumped into the ocean,
And swam like fish,
We caught some fish,
And set a fire to cook the fish and eat,
Once we ate, we went home,
And had a great time,
So they asked for a sleepover,
And they got it,
And they had the best time ever,
Best birthday ever.

Taylor Clarke (9)
Muirhouse Primary School, Motherwell

My Monster

My monster is in love with fashion,
My monster loves cuddles,
Cuddly is super friendly,
Cuddly is a fan of purple,
Cuddly has no friends,
Cuddly loves his spacecraft,
Cuddly hates the colour white,
Cuddly loves doughnuts,
Cuddly loves to keep his teeth clean,
Cuddly loves to fold clothes,
Cuddly is the heart of my life,
So please like Cuddly because he might come alive.

Olivia Speirs (9)
Muirhouse Primary School, Motherwell

Colourful One-Eyed Dragon

My monster is colourful,
My monster is a dragon,
My monster is a skateboarder,

My monster is from Scotland,
My monster is very nice,
My monster is very amazing,

My monster is lovely,
My monster is very responsible,
My monster is very good at skateboarding,

My monster is very good to other people,
My monster is caring,
My monster is always happy.

Ashton Warren (9)
Muirhouse Primary School, Motherwell

All About Tallulah

Tallulah, oh, she's so funny,
But she has no money,
Tallulah, she's a hairy little lady,
She's kinda small,
But also tall,
She's got fangs as sharp as a knife,
But she's got a good life,
Tallulah, Tallulah,
Ah, ah,
Tallulah, she's kinda goofy,
But she's awfully floofy,
Tallulah, ah, ah,
Tallulah!

Jenna Boyd (9)
Muirhouse Primary School, Motherwell

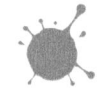

My Monster

My monster is named Gerald,
My monster is happy,
My monster is big and furry too,
His big antennae are bright yellow,
His cheeky personality isn't too good,
His big fangs chase everyone away,
But he has a big heart and that is good,
He may not be perfect, but he's my monster.

Max Kerr (10)
Muirhouse Primary School, Motherwell

Jimmy The Monster

My monster's name is Jimmy and he is a dragon,
My monster is a fire dragon that can fly and breathe fire and he's a really scary dragon,
My monster is the scariest dragon in all of the world and the universe,
My monster lives on Mars and there is a lot of fire and volcanos as well.

James Smillie (9)
Muirhouse Primary School, Motherwell

Chloe

My monster is soft,
My monster is purple and blue,
My monster likes dandelions,
My monster is kind,
My monster is called Chloe.

Chloe is popular,
Chloe is cute,
Chloe's best friend is called Jessica,
Chloe loves Jessica.

Caitlin Campbell (10)
Muirhouse Primary School, Motherwell

My Monster

My monster is spiky and sharp,
My monster has stinky breath and yellow teeth,
My monster is called Jessica,
Jessica is a good monster,
My monster isn't popular,
My monster, Jessica, only has one eye,
Jessica is blue and scary.

Emily Lindsay (9)
Muirhouse Primary School, Motherwell

Super Sandy

My monster is so happy,
Lighting up the world,
Not a single shadow to be seen,
My monster is so naughty, eating all my food,
Not even saying sorry to you,
Oh, little fluffball, what will we do with you?

Matilda Burnett (9)
Muirhouse Primary School, Motherwell

My Monster

My monster is brighter than the sun,
My monster is greener than the grass,
My monster has a big heart,
My monster could have the biggest of them all,
My monster is the most caring of them all.

Harry Brown (9)
Muirhouse Primary School, Motherwell

Shifter

There was a monster as horrible as the devil,
He was a shapeshifter,
His name was Shifter,
He hid under children's beds,
Shapeshifted to look like a family member,
And ate them!

James R (10)
Muirhouse Primary School, Motherwell

All About Dizzy

My monster is hairy,
My monster is very silly,
My monster is not that smart,
He wears ripped clothes,
He is very nice,
He sometimes eats treats.

Leland Dume (9)
Muirhouse Primary School, Motherwell

About Kenny

Kenny, as old as time,
Kenny, as strong as a brick wall,
Kenny, as flexible as a rubber band,
My monster is as hot as fire,
Yet as soft as cotton.

Zak Gilfillan (10)
Muirhouse Primary School, Motherwell

Rizzy Monster

One time, Rizzy fell into a hole,
He was stuck,
The hole was deep,
He broke his ankle,
He got out and went on.

Lewis Boyle (9)
Muirhouse Primary School, Motherwell

Monster Mars

I am a monster named Page,
I live on Mars and there are lots of chocolate bars,
I have three eyes and six sharp teeth,
I have freckles and I am very hairy,
I have powers and the powers are being invisible,
And I can fly, that's why I have two hairy wings,
I have eighteen friends,
I am very kind to people, so I can be good,
I would go to Saturn because it has lovely rings around it,
Also, I would love to go to Earth because lots of people are there,
I would love to eat Mars chocolate bars all day because it is my favourite,
I also look like a mermaid because I have a long tail,
I am also very cute and adorable.

Maryam Bilal (9)
Selwyn Primary School, London

Who Am I?

I am not a man, nor a hero,
I am not a woman, nor an angel,
People look at me and call me Death,
For I am immortal
I travel through portals,
But at day, I am just like you,
A mortal human being,
Working and reading,
But when the clock hits twelve,
I come alive,
Now is the hour you mortals most fear,
From a mere shadow,
A non-existent creature,
To huge claws and sharp teeth,
I hear your heart beating,
Thud! Thud! Thud!
I see your tears falling,
Splat! Splat! Splat!
You'd think it's over,
But the nightmare
Has just begun.

Amnah Hussain (9)
Selwyn Primary School, London

The Misunderstood

There was a hairy monster,
He was mighty and quick.
Everyone runs when they see
The monster that comes out from the sea.

The monster comes with a whole package,
Mighty talons,
Big, sharp teeth that he uses to eat.

This monster was Mr Misunderstood,
For everyone mistook him.

Mr Misunderstood cried and cried, for he never had a friend.
But one strange day, a boy stood still while the beast came to shore,
The little boy understood him and gave him a very big hug,
The monster made his first new friend and continued to get much more.

Kamran Fernandes (10)
Selwyn Primary School, London

Naughty Monster

My monster is a very naughty monster,
He fails in all of his exams,
Jack the monster doesn't care about anyone,
He is a five-eyed monster who is very hairy,
Jack likes to make people upset by pulling pranks,
Jokes, and backbiting,
He is rude, naughty, and scary,
Jack the monster should be in boarding school,
So he can learn how to be nicer,
Jack smiles every time he wants to pull a prank,
I know you're thinking that the naughty monster is going to plan something even worse this time,
That's why we should keep an eye out.

Fatima Diop (9)
Selwyn Primary School, London

The Cute-A-Dee

Where's the Cute-a-Dee?

Have you seen the Cute-a-Dee?
Peekaboo! There is she!
Mischievous as ever, whether you like it or not,
She's going to show you what she's got!

Pretty and petite,
Throws tantrums all the time,
Doesn't listen to her father, whose favourite food is lime.

She lives in a fairy world where everyone is free,
Because she is tiny,
She comes in on a bee,
Cute-a-Dee the tantrum queen!

"At least, that's what Daddy tells me,
Hehe!" says Cute-a-Dee.

Keona-May Jones (9)
Selwyn Primary School, London

Nogo The Bashful Monster

I am nice Nogo,
Flying high in the sky,
Singing sweet and loud,
But I am still not proud,
But not naughty either.

I am a playful monster,
When I'm tired, I take a breather,
But it only lasts a second,
That's why I get tired so easily,
But who cares?

People say I need to have more friends,
But I'm too scared,
My friends said I cared and shared,
But I still have five,
Which I think is enough.

Nusaiba Miah (9)
Selwyn Primary School, London

Puchy Is My Monster

Puchy is my monster,
A blob with a heart,
Her smile is pretty,
And her giggles are an art,
She is covered in pink fur,
And the sound that she makes is grr, grr!
She is kind to all, big and small,
And her favourite thing to do is use a ball,
She is my true friend
Who is always there,
And when I feel down,
She will show me she cares.

Ammarah Iqbal (9)
Selwyn Primary School, London

Monster

There might be some monsters
Under your bed,
Hairy, scary,
Or kind and calm ones,
But beware!
There could be monsters lurking in your room,
So turn the light on and make sure you are okay,
You might even see a friendly monster,
Orange, yellow or red,
Make sure you've got a friend,
A hairy scary monster might eat you!

Nijah Hossain (8)
Selwyn Primary School, London

All About Fleshy

I am not a human,
I am a monster,
I like to help people,
I look scary, but I am friendly,
I am a five-eyed monster,
I like to eat mango,
I like to drink strawberry milkshake,
My favourite sport is cricket.

Umar Chamdiya (10)
Selwyn Primary School, London

Space Squid

He jumps,
He takes his bike on a hike,
He flies a kite,
He's like a pilot in the sky,
He soars through the planets and catches them in his net,
He has them all to keep,
And he is Space Squid!

Ayaan Khan (8)
Selwyn Primary School, London

Fearsome Fang Finds A Friend

Once, in a land far away,
There roamed a mythical dragon called Fang.
He was scary, hairy, and fearsome.
In reality, he was lonely, friendly,
And longed for some company.
He loved helping the animals,
But they thought he was scary.
He would spend his day twisting and turning in the air,
Dreaming of someone for whom he could care.
Others thought he was frightening, a heart made of stone,
But, in fact, he was shy, and lonely he'd roam.
Until a bold hedgehog shrieked to the sky,
"Help me, please, dragon! I want to fly!"
He laid down his long tail, all fluffy and soft,
While shouting to hedgehog, "Of course, little one, climb aloft!"

Rosie Mellor (9)
St Austin's Catholic (VA) Primary School, Stafford

Monster ADHD

I have a little monster,
His name is ADHD,
When I least expect it,
He pokes fun at me.

He whirls around in my mind,
Making things a muddle,
He keeps me awake at night,
Making school mornings a struggle.

He's a proper little chatterbox,
This monster, ADHD,
He's constantly fidgeting,
And tapping on my knee.

He acts without thinking,
Sometimes getting me in trouble,
Interrupting conversations,
Popping that speech bubble.

I have a little monster,
His name is ADHD,
He is full of courage, high energy,
And is a very good friend to me.

He makes me hyper-focus
On things that I enjoy,
He can be positive,
This special little boy.

I wish the world would love him,
Just the same as me,
My little monster,
ADHD.

Darcy Bickford-Kehoe (8)
St Austin's Catholic (VA) Primary School, Stafford

Mermilicious

My monster is called Mermilicious,
And thinks seaweed is quite delicious.
She is big and strong,
But only lasts until the bell goes *bong!*
Mermilicious lives in the sea,
And saves sailors whose boats sank while they drank tea.
Her snake-like tail
Helps sailors to sail
To imaginary lands!
She also has two hands.
Mermilicious' craving for saving
Is the best job in the world!

Shreya Neelapala (9)
St Austin's Catholic (VA) Primary School, Stafford

Monster, Monster

Monster, monster, so, so green,
Monster, monster, so supreme,
Monster, monster, so, so fair,
Monster, monster, from your lair,
Monster, monster, so, so slimy,
Monster, monster, you're very grimy,
Monster, monster, what's your name?
Monster, monster, are you tame?
Monster, monster, coming closer,
Monster, monster, what a poser!

Niamh McNally (8)
St Austin's Catholic (VA) Primary School, Stafford

At Night

At night, it comes out,
At night, the Smiggle-Sprog comes,
At night, it chases people around,
At night, it roams the empty streets,
At night, it can hear you while you sleep.

When the time is six, get back to your house,
Before it's too late and the Smiggle-Sprog is awake!

Queenie Blewitt (9)
St Austin's Catholic (VA) Primary School, Stafford

The Terrible Twosome

James is a pain!
He moans about his extra toe,
He screams when he sees cups of tea.

Dotty is rather potty!
She eats a lot of different meats,
From a tin inside the bin.

They share one body!
But have their own thoughts,
They are the terrible twosome!

Talitha Chell (9)
St Austin's Catholic (VA) Primary School, Stafford

Snuggle

When it's late at night,
And dark and scary,
You need a friend,
So you won't be lonely.
Her name is Snuggle,
And she is there when you struggle.
She is soft and fluffy,
And never gets huffy,
Whether here or there,
Snuggle likes a huggle anywhere.

Annabelle-Faye Watts (9)
St Austin's Catholic (VA) Primary School, Stafford

The Acid Killer

Acid rain falls from the sky,
People, in fear, cry
As their loved ones die.
His enormous feet crush the town,
People fall to the ground.
The monster's mouth,
Like a black hole,
He could eat a train full of coal.

Tobias Smalley (9)
St Austin's Catholic (VA) Primary School, Stafford

Young Writers Information

We hope you have enjoyed reading this book – and that you will continue to in the coming years.

If you're the parent or family member of an enthusiastic poet or story writer, do visit our website www.youngwriters.co.uk/subscribe and sign up to receive news, competitions, writing challenges and tips, activities and much, much more! There's lots to keep budding writers motivated!

If you would like to order further copies of this book, or any of our other titles, then please give us a call or order via your online account.

Young Writers
Remus House
Coltsfoot Drive
Peterborough
PE2 9BF
(01733) 890066
info@youngwriters.co.uk

Join in the conversation!
Tips, news, giveaways and much more!

YoungWritersUK   YoungWritersCW   youngwriterscw

Scan me to watch the
Monster Poetry Video